I pray that hands and hearts that touch this book are inspired and encouraged by my life testimony through this book. Thanks Ms. Ermine

Jennifer Green

Single, Saved and Satisfied

(view of a saved single parent)

Written By

Jennifer Green

Single, Saved and Satisfied

(view of a saved single parent)

Copyright © 2016 by Jennifer Green

All rights reserved. No part of this book may be used or reproduced by any means, graphic, electronic, mechanical, including photocopying, recording, taping or by any information storage retrieval system without the written permission of the publisher except in the case of brief quotations embodied in critical articles and reviews.

ISBN 978-1-387-86276-4

Book Cover Illustrator- JBX Graphix- http://jbx-graphix.business.site

Printed in the USA

First Edition: May 2018

First and Foremost to God be the glory for the things he has done. To my Mother Helen Gandy, I love you so much and for showing me what it takes to be a strong, independent single parent. You have prayed encouraged and worked so hard to make sure that my siblings and I had a happy life. To my brother, my sisters and to my entire family love to you all.

This book is dedicated to my daughters Keiana and Ajana'e who has blessed my life in so many ways. To Pastor Tina Andrews who has always prayed and mentored me in becoming a great woman of faith. To Minister Roger G. McCloud who unselfishly prayed, encouraged me to go a little further. Who helped push me beyond my limits to believe in myself and the anointing of God upon my life. To God Almighty who in spite of my sin forgive, blessed and kept me when I felt that I was at my lowest point. Lord you comforted and blessed me. I'm eternally grateful and so overwhelm that I cannot even begin to explain how deeply, you have changed my life. Thank You

In Loving Memory of my sisters Ann and Sharon, my grandmother Iola and my stepfather Thomas Bill who although not being my biological father never ceased to treat me like his own.

Special thanks to Davilyn Campbell for her unselfish help and time in helping and creating a wonderful cover drawing of my girls.

Introduction

Someone asked me many years ago "Why don't you write a book about being a single parent?" So I began at times to jot down significant thought that came to mind about single parenthood from a Christian perspective. Those thoughts have now become this book in which you are about to read today.

I am the seventh child of Helen Gandy. I am the 1988 recipient of the Youth of the Year Award, The 1988 recipient of Humanitarian Award from Brooklyn Borough President Howard Golden, and the 2001 and 2005 Recognition of Achievement Award from Safe Horizon Organization. I am a dedicated and certified foster mother for seven years, retired from the New York City Police Department after 27 years of service and Owner of Iola's Grands Glitz, Glam and Glamour Party Planning Services. Most of all the proud single parent of two amazing daughters Keiana age 19 who has been my inspiration to go above and beyond to show her by example that hard work and determination go hand and hand, that she can fulfill all her dreams. Who's bright, sweet and always thinks about others before herself and Ajana'e age 4 Who is my ray of sunshine, with a bigger than life attitude who loves and is compassionate about everything and everybody. Her presence can light up anybody's day with a smile that will always warm your heart.

My motto is: "If I can help somebody as I pass along then my living shall not be in vain." I accepted Jesus Christ as my Lord and Savior on April 24, 1981, and experienced the baptism of the Holy Ghost manifest by speaking in tongues on September 2, 1983 under the Leadership of the late Father Connie Mobley Pastor of the United Community Baptist Church in Coney Island. Most happily I rededicated my life to Christ in 2006 under the leadership of the late Elder Eric T. Miller Pastor of the Beulah Church of Christ, Coney Island

Contents

Introduction

Chapter 1	The Single Parent
Chapter 2	Relationships
Chapter 3	What Is Your Ministry?
Chapter 4	Who Told You, You Were Naked?
Chapter 5	Forgiveness
Chapter 6	Staying Focused
Chapter 7	Lord, You Are The Potter, I Am The Clay
Chapter 8	Fulfillment
Chapter 9	Releasing Everything From Our Past
Chapter 10	The Promise

Chapter 11	Envision Finding Our Way Back
Chapter 12	Can I Breathe?
Chapter 13	A Look Through My Daughter's Eyes
Chapter 14	Can The Church Say Amen, Celebrate The New You

Single Parents Quotes

My Personal Reflections

A Single Parent Prayer Letter To God

Inspire, Encourage and Uplift

The Single Parent

Who said that being a single parent is hard? Not me! It is however at times a little challenging and hectic: from finding a reliable babysitter to getting to work on time. *Jeremiah 1:5 says "before you were formed in the belly I knew thee."*

Anyone who has given birth to a child or raising children on his or her own might have felt the way I did. Will my child look like me? Who else might they resemble in the family? Will she have my smile and will she have my great sense of humor?

My daughter's father chose not to be a part of her life in doing so he missed the opportunity of raising an amazingly, intelligent, sweet lovable young lady. (Keiana I Love You.) Let me be honest at first I was bitter, and frustrated but I learned that I can do all things through Christ who strengthens me. Yes I sinned sexuality outside the marriage covenant were my errors before God and with a married man, yes married. I can admit it now and thank God for his forgiveness and his mercy I could have died in my sins but God saw fit to give me a second chance.

I want someone who is going through this now to learn to forgive and forget and move on because if not you will never live the life God has planned for you. God can do above and beyond all we could ever think or hope, that's why I love him so much. If you keep sin covered or bottled up its hindering you.

Being a single parent does not mean your life is over actually, the fun has just begun! You can share and instill into your children so much knowledge, wisdom and a foundation of knowing who God is and everything He's promised to be. The foundation has to be laid out for our children to strive to do and be all that they can be, we are shaping leaders and not just followers. Take the time to spend with your children just to sit down and chat sometimes. Children who are comfortable in their environment and loved want to talk and are not afraid to speak about anything. This is what builds a strong relationship between you and your children. Let them see there's more to life than just your inner circle. Let them experience life beyond your reach.

Remember you don't have to strive to be both parents. Stay in your lane just be a mom or dad. God will make up for what's missing. *Proverbs 22:6 states train up a child the way he should go, and when he is old, he will not depart from it.*

Single parents are no longer defined by our circumstances God is with us. Being a Christian does not mean all your problems will magically disappear or that you will always point your children to Jesus who is ever ready to bless us.

Ponder on this: Does a son want his father to sit in the stands at his basketball games, or a daughter want her mother's advice during her first days as she comes of age? Does a daughter want her mother to show her how to be beautiful or does she want her dad to take her to her "Father-Daughter dance?"

Does a daughter need her father to say that she's daddy's girl only, or does a son needs his dad to show him how to shave and how to treat a lady right. - The answer is Yes to all of the above and much more!

Some people always say I can't help him be a man. My answer is yes you can, who says you can't. Teach your son that true manhood is being responsible and not running away from accountability. Don't look for validation in the streets, men have flaws and issues - God does not.

A little humor: I know sometimes, your child or children can get on your last nerve and they do. We deal with it because we cannot send them back to where they came. A lot of ladies will be gasping and crying head first. OH MY, MY, MY - NO MA'AM

Chapter 2
Relationships

Oh boy! Where do I begin? Let me start by saying if you're dating be sure to maintain your virtue. In short, we can't be saved on Sunday and lose our salvation on Monday!!!

In dating relationships, you have to be very careful as to whom you allow in your life. My mistake was coming over just to spend time and watch a movie (we all know that one). Most of us say I want a good man or woman a true believer. We miss it that salvation starts from the heart not your head.

That's why I can tell you thank God for deliverance. It's the heart relationship of our spirit with Christ that must be in order first then we can prosper in other areas of our life.

If you desire to be married waiting can be hard, use this time to find those areas in yourself that need healing, freedom and growth. Work on you and your life with the Lord fully find your rest in him. Learn to trust him and wait upon his provision for

Galatians 6:9 says And let us not get weary in doing well: for in due season we shall reap, if we faint not.

Pursuing relationships has the potential at times to cause you to go astray from your primary purpose as a single parent which is raising your children in a Godly environment in a Godly way.

You want what's best for your children persistence to lock into numerous relationships can be disastrous. Waiting on God is beautiful. It is paramount.

Lastly God is faithful to meet our every need bringing fulfillment to you and your children. In his eyes delay is not denial. Keep trusting him through this.

Proverbs 3:5-6 says trust in the Lord with all thine heart and lean not unto thy own understanding, in all thy ways acknowledge him and he will direct your path.

Suppose you're out on a date and you stop to bless your food and when you do, you look up to see the other individual with their head bowed too. Perhaps on the next date you may want to find out where his or her heart lies. Or were they by chance waiting for you to finish with their fork in their hand. You might want to rethink things. What would be your next remark? Remember my comment about delay. God is teaching us how to wait. Not Yet. Keep trusting God.

A little humor: When you go out on a date you can't wait for your date to go to the restroom, so once they stepped away from the table you can really eat "I know I should have not ordered this salad." "I'm hungry." That's what you're telling yourself (smile). Remember the key word companion-dating is companionship not relationship be careful.

Chapter 3
What Is Your Ministry?

I want to live so that God can use me anytime and anywhere

I realized that my ministry was to sing, while attending a church in my youth I was unexpectedly called to render a solo. Yes, I was beyond nervous because I never considered myself a soloist, not even a lead singer but, God had a plan for me. I thank him for choosing me and not me choosing myself.

Consider this:

1. **Every Christian has a gift.** 1Peter 4:10 says every Man hath received the gift even so minister that Same one to another, as good stewards of the Manifold grace of God. **Knowing them shapes your Calling.**

2. **If you feel sincere compassion to minister to others**

3. **Pray to God to use you generously**

4. **Listen humbly to spiritual people in your life.**

If God called you, he will equip you and fill you so that you may be poured out for others. So, your ministry can be one of many like helping other single parents, teenage mothers, runaway youth, or even the elderly. Sometimes people just need an ear to listen to than somebody judging them. Even when our steps seem to be not quite in the right direction trust that God is faithfully guiding us.

God calls us all to service far beyond anything you could ever think or imagine. You we're put on earth to make a contribution. If you are a Christian, you are a minister of God's grace and when you're serving you are ministering. God designed you to make a difference by your life.

Isaiah 6:8 says Then I heard the voice of the Lord saying "Whom shall I send, and who will go for us?" Then I said "Here I am send me".

A little humor: You're at service trying to help the sister with the bad children, and one just stomped on your toe, stuck their tongue out at you and, just told you you're not my mother. While you're walking away with a smile on your face and you say to yourself. "Oooohh my toe"!!!

Chapter 4

Who Told You, You Were Naked?

We assume that no one is going to see the scars of our past so we clothe ourselves in all the name brands and makeup just to mask our human frailty. We are afraid of being exposed and uncovered in regards to the person that we are in reality.

Matthew 25:36 Naked, and ye clothed me

In Genesis It's Adam who felt that he was not good enough. He felt that he was damaged goods and unworthy of

God's love. We too may feel robbed and that our relationship with God is damaged. God says however that you are blessed, chosen, blameless and redeemed through his blood and with certainty and no fear, shame or guilt. You are totally his own, completely forgiven and most of all not forgotten.

Naked we feel that we're not worthy to receive God's blessings because of our past. We feel that we have no value, no self esteem, no self worth. To God however you are worth more than anything in this world. You may feel that you don't matter but once you accept the realities of being a single parent. You begin the process of covering up the shame and the blame. You may have ostracized yourself, and remained at arm's length from the presence of God. He is concerned about you and your life and wants to make you feel whole.

In God's eyes, it doesn't matter how many times you've fallen ask him to cover you with his glory for he has healed your broken past. You feel people will look at you and judge you, making you feel inadequate. God's process of you receiving healing not just putting a band aid on it, but healing from the inside out from the root when it's your season no one can stop or block your blessings.

When your children fall and get a scratch or cut they call you to fix it and put a band aid on it. They truly desire your help until they feel ashamed because of the other children in the park, or school will see and tease them and call them a baby. What would your reply be? Would you not reply, "who told you that you were a baby?" I covered you because you are loved!

Passion or Compassion Empathy for Sympathy Release or Relieve Progress or Process Reborn or Rebirth

Chapter 5
Forgiveness

"You hurt me, I thought you were going to be there to help me raise our child. At first you seem to want to be there only because that's what your parents wanted NOT YOU! It wasn't about your relationship with me but our child, STOP and think about it she needed you from day one however, We Forgive You". Have you ever envisioned these very words or thoughts like them as you addressed the absent parent in your child's life?

Matthew 18:21-22 Then came Peter to him and said, Lord how oft shall my brother sin against me, and I forgive him? Till seven times? Jesus saith unto him, I say not unto thee, Until seven times: but, Until seventy times seven.

We always ask God to forgive us but when it comes to our heart we find it hard for us to forgive others. We can't live a peaceful life if we're still holding on to bitterness, resentment towards others. God's grace helps us do things easily that would otherwise be hard. Forgiveness is a process it takes time to release a painful past. Unforgiveness keeps us in the past and in bondage. An unwillingness to forgive will keep you in your own prison of personal pain and sickness. God desires our suffering to cease. He therefore commends to break down the walls or bitterness so that we can forgive and live.

Matthew 6:14 For if you forgive men their trespasses, your heavenly Father will also forgive you.

Even though it's difficult it means letting go of something. What is done is done and can't be undone but, forgiveness is FREEDOM of resentment and grudges. We can exercise the willpower to forgive and pray for the person that caused you pain this takes the power that others had over you away and give you your life back. You can have a clean slate and live from a place of growth.

Only the power of the Holy Spirit within us can enable us to fully forgive those who have hurt us. Is there anyone you need to forgive? Or someone who you need to apologize to? Do It Today!!!

Chapter 6
Staying Focused

I press towards the mark for the prize of the high calling of God in Christ Jesus. Philippians 3:14

Sometimes bad things happen to good people. Such is life therefore it's not the fact as to whether or not your life is problem free, but how you handle trouble when it comes. Don't be discouraged "for greater is he that is in me than he that is in the world". From God's perspective trials come to build our faith. Remember don't lose your faith for after the rain God sends a rainbow. Don't give in or give up. This reminds me of a song that my pastor the late Elder Eric T Miller would sing "When my heart is overwhelmed lead me to the rock that is higher than I, higher than I".

Single parents your testimony can reach someone that's at the end of their rope. People interact with us daily and yet do not really know us. We become afraid to telling our story. You can never really mature as a believer until you let go of the fear of sharing your testimony and the gospel of Jesus Christ. When you express your beliefs, it opens up a door for someone else to receive their healing. Remain without excuses, don't let anyone defer you from sharing the good news.

Let's take a look through the Bible and

discover the saints who God used and why he gave them a new focus.

Abraham **was old and did use excuses** Jacob **was insecure** Leah **was unattractive** Joseph **was abused**

Moses **stuttered** Gideon **was poor** Samson **was codependent** Rahab **was immoral**

David **had an affair and had all kinds of family problems** Elijah **was suicidal** Jeremiah **was depressed** Jonah **was reluctant**

Naomi **was a widow** Peter **was impulsive and hot tempered** The Samaritan Woman **had several failed marriages** Thomas **had doubts**

God used each of them in his service and he is ready to use you too. Remember our children will learn how to depend on God as we learn through his mercies to overcome our shortcomings, weaknesses, and past to fulfill the call of God upon your life

There will be bumps, detours, blocked exits but continue to walk strong with your shoulders up and head held high because, once

God is finished with you. You shall come out as pure gold, yes through it all God is faithful and just.

Some suffer from tunnel vision and lack of ability to see a broad view However, when you come to the realization that the world does not revolve around you. Your focus is no longer obscure, you no longer find it difficult for people to love and understand you or for you to understand them.

Think on this: You're driving home from work, church or school and it begins to rain buckets as if God opened up the windows of heaven. Your wipers, fog defrost is on but, you still have to wipe your windows from the inside because your vision has become foggy. Focus your vision for what seems to be clouding your mind like now the children are growing up and you finally can start going back to school to further your education, writing a book or starting your own business. Let your focus be the same pleasing God. Release the haze, blurry and cloudy vision that is clouding your mind and stay focused on what's to come. Be Bless

Chapter 7
Lord, You are The Potter and I am the Clay

We are molded and shaped by God

But now, O Lord, thou art our father; we are the clay, and thou our potter, and we all are the work of thy hand.

(Isaiah 64:8)

Mold (to give shape or form) Shaped (outlined) Form (create or produce) Biblically (form thee - gave birth)

Isaiah 43:7 Even every one that is called by my name: for I have created him for my glory, I have formed him; yea, I have made him.

Have you ever seen a potter working with fresh clay? That's how God has us in his hands. He shapes our character just as the potter does with the clay. God knows exactly who we are. God sees our hearts. He is the all seeing one. He forgives, heals and sets us free. Be patient God isn't finished with us yet. We are a work in progress.

The Bible says that we are to grow in the knowledge of God, and

One of the main ways that you will grow in the knowledge of God is to read his word. The reason why so many of God's children are not spiritually growing is because, they are not spending quality time with God by reading and understanding the word of God. Just like a potter cannot use the clay unless there is enough water - God cannot start molding, shaping until we start getting enough of his word in us.

Children often don't know how their parents stay up at night for them when they're ill. Praying fervently for their spiritual covering and asking God to bless especially at the times of feeling discouraged, sad and hurt.

I may be telling my age here, but I remember when I was in Junior High School there were sessions you might remember called "Shop" classes. Where you can pick which class that you wanted to attend such as: woodshop, ceramics, sewing class and cooking. Some of my classmates picked ceramics where they learned how to mold, shape clay and seal it, for when it's done they could see what they created. Some of us want to do mold and shape our own destiny in the same manner. We want control of our entire life process from beginning to end. God however is in full control of the process, he will reshape and mold us over and over again. We like little children must learn to trust him and yield to his creativeness within us.

Think on this: God's hand literally goes deep down into our soul and spirit to mold and transform us. At times, it can become painful and unpleasant while God is removing all the negative qualities while at the same time instilling and imparting all of the good, positive and Godly qualities that he wants us to have.

Stay focused for great is your reward

in heaven. No one can tear down what God has built up in you. No one but yourself can stop your growth and hinder what God has planted in you. So, commit yourself to the process of yielding to God by pure worship. "Blessed are the pure in heart for they shall see God". As the Lord shapes us and mold us His image begins to appear upon us. Those all around us no longer see our physicality but rather they behold Christ who abides within us by His Holy Spirit. What a wonderful thing to be transformed by God!! Lord you are the potter, I am the clay grant us the grace to yield to the process for your glory!

Chapter 8
Fulfillment

And Jesus said unto them, I am the bread of life: he that cometh to me shall never hunger; and he that believeth on me shall never thirst (John 6:35)

Do you want fulfillment? Does your heart cry out for deep satisfaction take a moment to drink the life giving principles of the word of God - the water of life your heart will thank you for it.

Think of a stormy day of which you cannot go outside, so you have family time indoors after you've played so many games and nothing good is on the television to watch. You come to appreciate this quality time with your children such as:

*Laying across the bed talking, laughing then everyone falls asleep, only to wake up and see the children still napping.

*In silence, you start thanking God for all the things that God has provided such moments are necessary they remind us that all is well. King Jesus is still on the Throne.

*That love is our greatest possession and the future is nothing to fear.

*We can count our blessings moments of peace (minutes of relaxation like sipping on your favorite cup of tea).

*Prayer and devotional time (for me it's when my daughters are at school or time alone in my bedroom).

*During the holiday season at Christmas time sitting in the living room in the dark watching the twinkling lights from the tree.

As believers, we find fulfillment through obedience to God. We cannot find fulfillment in people, places or things. It can only be found as we walk in obedience to the will of God for our lives.

Is God trying to get your attention? Do you realize he is your first love? God wants an intimate relationship with you first before you can seek an intimate relationship with anyone. Intimacy with God connotes time with him reading and praying his word into your spirit knowing that he is your comforter. It's entering into rest- leaning and depending upon him who will keep your deepest secrets. God himself is the source of true fulfillment.

Think on this: Have you ever gone out to eat at your favorite restaurant and, ordered your favorite dish and asked for a double portion of something on your plate? I know I have. This is what God wants for us that we might receive a double portion of his heart and presence.

Isaiah 61:7 says for your shame ye shall have double; for confusion they shall rejoice in their portion: therefore in their land they shall possess double: everlasting joy shall be unto them.

Chapter 9
Releasing Everything From Our Past

What was it that wounded your spirit? What made you bitter? What made you stop believing?

The answer to these questions is invite God into that hidden part of yourself right now, take him right to the place where you died inside.

Past relationships, bitter divorce, friendships that have caused hurt when you thought it was a lasting one. Situations and circumstances that transpired into a negative cause of great pain. I have had relationships and friendships that I thought would never end but unfortunately it wasn't for me. God places certain people in our lives to help and comfort us but, when things really began to fall apart, how quickly you find that people change. I've learned that some people are only in your life for a season. Through the years I've learned that God will remove everything

and everyone that's not good for you or healthy for your well being.

You were created with a purpose and a destiny God's best work still lies ahead

of you. Do not allow your circumstances past or present to get the best of you. Allow God to take what the enemy meant for your harm, and use it for your good. *Proverbs 31:10-12, 28-31 says Who can find a virtuous woman? for her price is far above rubies. The heart of her husband doth safely trust in her, so that he shall have no need of spoil. She will do him good and not evil all the days of her life. Her children arise up and call her blessed; her husband also, and he praiseth her. Many daughters have done virtuously, but thou excellest them all. Favour is deceitful and beauty is vain: but a woman that feareth the Lord, she shall be praised. Give her of the fruit of her hands; and let her own works praise her in the gates.*

One important key in life is releasing the past. What you are most

passionate today will be birthed tomorrow. Bury your past and allow yourself to let God birth his plan in your life. Do not let your past continue to control your future by reliving it. You're giving it more power over your life than you deserve you are so much stronger than that. There will be some relationships that

must be removed from your life before you can inherit what God has for you.

Think on this: Sometimes things from our past can be embarrassing, upsetting and can cause great pain if someone finds out. That thing you buried in your past. Your past is your past God had already healed and delivered you from it you therefore release it! You will see you have grown stronger more than you or they ever known.

Release Letting go everything from my past **Revive** Living in the daily presence of God **Renewed** Shaking off the old ways and begin a new walk in Christ **Reverence** Thanking God for all things **Regenerate** Newfound strength, to go on it spite of my past **Reborn** Beginning a new life **Repent** Admitting your faults and reclaim your inheritance

Find the Princess or Prince that you are. Recognize that you were born into greatness. Your father is the Most High King, walk in your inheritance that is yours. When you're confident and acknowledge that you don't have to take the devil's mess. You'll

never revisit your hurtful past

anymore. Send guilt and shame back to where it came from for there is no condemnation to them who are in Christ Jesus.

Chapter 10
The Promises

Promises, Promises, Promises

He said, "Baby I promise I will never hurt you again, I promise I'll make it better!" She said, "Honey I promise I will never speak to him again, I promise I'll delete his number."

Don't make a promise you can't keep.

I remember when I was young and shopping with my mother when I'd seen something in the store I wanted. I asked my mother "Mom can I get this" she would reply If you promise that when we get home you will do this or that. My reply was yes only to get home and forget all what I had promised.

Believers who are (single parents) must cling on to God's promise that he is indeed able to do exceedingly abundantly above all that

we ask or think....Take some time and think on that. What a loving God we serve.

Hebrews 6:12 The promises of God are inherited through faith and patience. **If God promised you something, it will come to pass. Many of us throw in the towel and quit just before our breakthrough. The enemy is a master at sending distractions into your life to take your eyes and focus off God. BEWARE AND TAKE CAUTION!!!**

The decisions we make that are life changing should not be based upon how we feel. Feelings change constantly, your emotions can be deceptive. God will always appoint a time of healing and restoration for you. While you're waiting God is working. Don't think that the season of waiting means that God has stopped working. No, He's just taking you through that season because he's using the time to work in your life for your good.

Think on this: We all have made promises that we know we couldn't keep. You know the saying: "God I promise if you get me out of this..." Thank God for his promise that he will never leave or forsake us. This a truth that we can bank on. God always keeps his promises whatever he says

HE WILL DO - STAND ON IT.

He is watching. You may be asking "when Lord?" God is saying "Will you trust me through this".

Someone you loved may have told you, "I love you and I promise I will never cheat, hurt or abuse you". Was it love or just infatuation? Did you discover that what you'd seen and loved on

the outside was nothing about what's on the inside. Nobody told me he was a batterer, or that she was an alcoholic. No one prepared you for the gambler who just lost his job now you have to take care of him. By moving so quickly into the relationship only afterwards you realize it was never what God intended for you. You thought that he or she was a keeper and the sad part about the entire relationship is that your children who are the most important persons in the world to you are caught up in the midst of it.

Chapter 11
Envision Finding Our Way Back

Envision - To see ahead or conceive something your heart desires.

Are you believing and waiting on God to see what he's going to do in your life? Keep the faith God is in control and has a plan.

Have you ever wished that you could start your life all over again? God wants to help us recover to experience a different kind of life in Christ Jesus.

The circumstance that people thought

would tear you down God kept you strong through it, the Lord knowing the vision that he had already placed in you. You had many obstacles but never sought revenge. Why? It's because you knew that God has a plan for your life. Being a single parent didn't break your faith even though we asked God "Why". God was in every situation guiding and directing us. We may never understand it completely however, we can be sure that the Lord is working it out.

Genesis 50:21 read on this wise: "Now therefore fear ye not: I will nourish you and your little ones. And he comforted them, and spake kindly unto them."

We get in the way of God's timing and miss out on our blessings. We have to learn how to love so we can experience the fullness of God's heart during our season of singleness. Everything will fall into place and it will be worth the wait. So, keep your vision clear finding your way back. God reveals his vision when he knows we are ready and able to receive it.

I remember at one time I had several different pairs of contacts lens that I would wear. One day I went to work while, at work I rubbed my eyes not only to find out my contacts moved, but that I had to dig in my eye to find it, once I did my vision became very blurry and I couldn't clear my vision until I removed both contacts. That's how God wants us to see our vision clearly without digging around to find it.

Finding our way back to God becomes

easy once we take our focus off what we think we have to do to get there. Some of us are still searching for answers about life but God has been searching for us for a long time. He wants you to find him too. As a single parent at times we seem to experience a void in our lives because of raising our children alone may cause us to feel inadequate. This often creates an emotional gap in our lives, affecting our growth and development mentally, emotionally and spiritually. Pick up, dust off your bible and you will feel God calling you back home. His arms are already wide open waiting for you to come.

Think on this: You're out shopping with your children you realize one of your children is missing so, you cry out his or her name and her nothing in return. You're walking around looking and searching to find them and begin to panic wondering where your child is. Until you hear their voice calling mommy or daddy where are you? God wants us to cry out in the same way and envision our way back. All the time he was looking and waiting for your call so he can welcome you back. Envision yourself running back to God his arms are wide open waiting to receive you.

Chapter 12

Can I Breathe?

Inhale, Exhale Breathe In, Breathe Out

I remember a few years ago when I had undergone a surgery, two hours afterwards in recovery I could hear the anesthesiologist repeatedly say breathe, breathe. Beloved that's exactly what God wants us to do breathe in as it were his Holy presence.

The purpose of our lives as single or married is the same. We were created to praise God whether things are rough or smooth we were created to praise Him in good times or bad.

YOU CAN BREATHE

Day after day as we live we have the opportunity to thank God for brand new mercies. We serve a God who understands. However, you may praise him whether with outstretched arms, clapping or with a whisper it still honors God.

Our daily motivation should always be the same Thank You Jesus I'm "breathing" for the covering of my children

for health and strength for making a way for release, revive, repair and rebuilding

Learn to release the things you cannot

control, step in the way with God and breathe.

Jeremiah 29:11-14 reminds us to BREATHE Message bible reads on this wise "As soon as Babylon's seventy years are up and not a day before, I'll show up and take care of you as I promised and bring you back home. I know what I'm doing. I have it all planned out plans to take care of you, not abandon you, plans to give you the future you hope for. "When you call on me, when you come and pray to me, I'll listen when you come looking for me, you'll find me. Yes, when you get serious about finding me and want it more than anything else, I'll make sure you won't be disappointed" God's Decree. I'll turn things around for you I'll bring you back from all the countries into which I drove you. God's Decree bring you home to the place from which I sent you off into exile". You can count on it.

Can I breathe, without you criticizing me? Can I breathe, without you keep bringing up my past? Can I breathe,

and raise my children? Can I breathe, let go and let God? Can I breathe, and meditate on God? Can I breathe, when I'm feeling overwhelmed?

As single parents each day by the word of God, we breathe life into the situations and circumstances that we go through. We let go of the past hurt, pain and move forth in the newness of Christ. Don't walk in the flesh! Begin to change all your thoughts and the focuses of your heart remain faithful as you meditate on God. Apply your heart each day to walk in God's favor in forgiveness, no complaining, no regrets.

For mothers who have ever given birth to a child remembers after all the pain and tears to see the baby you birthed take their first breathe is the sign a new life has begun. God is there when we are hurting. He knows. When we cried, he cried with us. Waiting for us to realize that he was birthing something in us so great.

You make me Happy You make me Laugh You make me Dance

You make me Sing You make me Shine And most of all BREATHE

Chapter 13
A Look Through My Daughter's Eyes

In this chapter I let my daughter speak on what it's like being a child of a single parent. I encourage you to read this chapter to your children to inspire and encourage them.

I introduce my oldest daughter Keiana Jana'e Green

My definition of a father one who begets his child. My definition of a dad one who provides and teaches you values.

Coming to terms with knowing that my father was never going to be in my life, caused me to feel alone. It was like he left one of his luggage at the airport and didn't bother to go back for it. That luggage was me, abandoned wondering what did I do wrong for him not wanting to be around me. After years of blaming myself for not having a relationship with my father. I came to the realization that it was not my fault, he is missing out on the amazing things I'm achieving. It's unfortunate that it's come to this, but God has plans that will benefit us in the end. Once you lose something, you become truly grateful for what you do have. I'm grateful to God and my mom, they have filled in those empty gaps he left in my heart.

Mom you are more than my mom, you are my advice giver, comedian, personal chef, doctor, stylist, movie buddy, and most importantly my best friend. There is never a dull moment between us but she will lay down the law when necessary. She puts my sister and I her number two priority for God is her first.

Even though I'm getting older and living in a single parent home I'm as blessed as someone that lives in a two parent home and I'm loving every minute of it. Growing up without a father does not define who I am, I've learned and am still learning that life without him does not dictate or influence who I am, I was born into greatness. Full time student attending Borough of Manhattan Community College majoring in forensic science, big sister to one of the most caring and loveable little sister in the world Ajana'e (who is sometimes a little bully). I love her so much.

What onlookers do not see is that I'm not damaged goods. Please don't pity me, I'm well-balanced and happy. God knew what was best for me.

My Poem Keiana Then and Now

Do You Love Me? I Don't See It but I Forgive You? Where Are You, I'm Crying but You Can't See My Tears Can We Talk? But You Don't Answer

These were the times when I knew you didn't care. Some people say out of sight, out of mind. I believe that's true. How can I get through this, Oh nobody told you? God carried me, wiped my tears, repaired my broken heart, restored my joy and loves me more.

1 Timothy 5:8 (NIV) says If anyone does not provide for his relatives and especially for his immediate family, he had denied the faith and is worse than an unbeliever.

Father's, Mother's take care of your children. What's the use of shouting, speaking in tongue or preaching when you are not taking care of your children. You might as well stop you are worse than a thief. I think that sums it up.

Chapter 14
Can The Church Say Amen, Celebrate The New You

Today is the day you release all the hurt and pain within your "shopping" list of issues.

Enter into your prayer closet and feel the presence of the Lord that is surrounding you. Thank him for making you whole, Thank him for who he is to you, Thank him for restoration and restoring, Thank him for salvation, Thank him for seeing you free from all the hurt, the pain and the worry. Through prayer, worship and praise take back everything-I mean everything that the enemy has stolen from you. Take back your sanity, your joy, your children,

your family, your peace, your finances. Begin to thank God for your deliverance. Just watch God open up the windows of heaven and pour you out a blessing that you will not have enough room to receive it.

When you let go and let God do it all, turn to the next chapter of your life. Find that person in you that has been buried, put on your best dress or finest suit, then go out and enjoy what God has resurrected in your life. Walk in favor! See a brand new you! Smile be zealous and experience a different walk.

Here's a short exercise I'd like you to participate in. Single parents reading this part if you're a male change woman to man and to "Ms. Right Now". Please review the following story and give it a try:

There was a young single woman with two children who have gave her all in her relationships, children, her family. Working hard to maintain her life and stability until she met "Mr. Right Now". This woman thought that he was perfect but instead she let him drag her down. He beat and humiliated her. Where could this mom go? Her life soon became filled with worry and fear. Slowly she began attending services sporadically, just to satisfy "Mr. Right Now" who would say "You don't have to go today stay home and spend time with me". She neglected fellowship with the saints and her Lord. Now she is downtrodden, discouraged and mentally unstable from all "Mr. Right Now" had done to her. She did not realize that the man who could comfort her as she was at her lowest point was there all the time his name is Jesus! Therefore, she struggled in every aspect in her life experiencing no joy, no peace, no sanity he had took all that from her. Now she is too preoccupied with pleasing "Mr. Right Now" who had taken away from her everything. She lost her focus on maintaining her home, children, and stability only to discover at the end that "Mr. Right Now" moved on without her. Her life has spiraled. How can she get back to where she used to be? If this were you what would you do? In the lines below how would you speak to this woman? Put yourself in her shoes for a moment after you've commented your view to this woman turn back to this chapter read what you written and encourage yourself!

_____
_____
_____
_____
_____
_____
_____

What does it mean to celebrate a new me? Totally surrendering your all to God. Letting him shape and form you. Your mind is clear, no more negative thinking, no longer accepting the enemy's lies. "Greater is he that is in me than he that is in the world". It's accepting the things from your past you can't change but looking forward to a great future in Christ.

Hello The New Me

In celebrating the new you don't become self-centered or self-righteous. Celebrate the new you through worship and fellowshipping with God. Walk in the Fruit of the **Spirit** *Galatians 5:22-23 "But the fruit of the spirit is love, joy, peace, forbearance, kindness, goodness, faithfulness, gentleness and self-control. Against such things there is no law".*

Let's pray:

Lord, I'm celebrating the new me knowing that I can't change my past but, I'm learning from it. Change is always good for when I'm changing I'm learning to let you change me from the inside out. In your son Jesus name Amen. I challenge you today make that first step in walking in the new YOU!

To Inspire Encourage And Uplift

As single parents, regardless of the path that has brought us here, this is for you, so you know that you do not have to walk alone. We share the same heart, same struggles and the same needs.

Sometimes we get to a place in our lives when we feel there is no one else, no place to go, we can't fix it, change it or reverse it, nothing left to believe. TRY CHRIST

Affirm:

We as single parents have the ability to create a good life for ourselves and our children. We are more than our circumstances; our possibilities are endless for every setback leads to a comeback.

Devote:

We see ourselves strong, smart, think big and dream bigger. Develop a vision for yourselves, be grateful for everything triumph and victory. Start seeing anew.

Pledge:

Today I'm going to make better choices for me and my child/children. Celebrate yourself and keep on no matter what.

Reflect:

On what comes to your mind about yourself and your future.

Submission:

Talk to God. This is bigger than me so I put it into your hands.

Expectancy:

We have not because we expect not. Remember ALL things work together for good. Our pain becomes his possibility.

Thankfulness:

Can we thank God while beating ourselves up? Turn your mourning into dancing and your sorrows into joy. We are clothed with God's favor therefore spiritually in him we are dressed for success.

God brings beauty out of the ruins of our past. He will not abandon you. Not knowing what lies ahead can be frightening leaving you feeling exposed and helpless. You may feel the future may be out of your hands, but it's not out of God's hands.

*If you know someone that needs a little encouragement. Share this page. Grace and Peace to you all.

Single Parent Daily Quotes

1. You don't have to fake it, you're going to make it.
2. When you bless somebody, you're blessing yourself.
3. Keep the faith the moment you think about giving up your Breakthrough is just about to begin.
4. Nobody has the power over you but God, he has equipped you with much more than you know. Walk in It.
5. Stay charged up even when you think you're Empty your Hidden strength is waiting to Restore

you.
6. See it, claim it, receive it, take a deep breath and enjoy all the blessings God has blessed you with healthy children, beautiful family and a prosperous God given life.
7. Quote 7 and God's divine number of completeness and perfection. Seven amazing characteristics of a single parent strong, independent, hardworking, caregiver, counselor and your number 1 cheerleader
8. The more people talk about you the more God keeps blessing keep talking-I know I'm blessed
9. They crucified Jesus so why not you hold on to everything God has given you for you're going to win. The bible says the race is

not given to the swift but to the one who endures to the end.

10. When you're looking and looking trying to find a way out STOP just look up and see JESUS.

11. I'm weak but I'm humbled when I'm feeling distorted I'm standing strong I'm perplexed but I'm figuring it out. These are the times when I say I want more, more of you Lord.

12. When I thought all hope was lost, you sent a rainbow when I asked you gave me so much more when I cried, my tears you wiped when I stumbled, you picked me up.

13. God's solution is plain: Don't

repress it, confess it, Don't conceal it, Reveal it.

14. This journey does not define who I am, it re-direct my purpose.

15. Walking through this tunnel is not giving me tunnel vision, because I see a bigger picture. Thank you, Jesus,

16. Don't window your dreams. Don't just look through it, open the window.

Personal Reflections

What about your past? Are you ready to let it go? Give it a graveyard burial do not resurrect it. Your tomorrow does not have to be like your yesterday, stop using what happened in your past to determine what will be your future.

It's easy to wiggle out of a small space once you've removed the layers of hurt, pain, discouragement that have draped your soul and what you have hidden beneath scars and brokenness. Don't let your scars fester let them heal.

On the space below write a promissory note to yourself specifying the issues of your past that you will no longer allow to affect your present and future.

I(Your Name)_____promise to release_____from my past. Lord I ask that you change me from the inside out and my future is not determined by my past. Thank you for new beginnings.

Repent	What I did was sin
Forgiveness	God forgiven you, now you can forgive yourself
Re-Evaluate God	Live your life fully to
Petition	Ask God to help you

Single Parent Prayer

Gracious God our Father we come to you broken, confused, perplexed, overwhelmed and needing your strength and guidance, knowing we haven't crossed every "T" and dotted every "I" but I know that you can restore, rebuild, revive protect and inspire me. Remove every chain that has held me back from receiving all that you have for me. I command them to be broken in the name of Jesus. Lord you know all about me and the difficulties that I face. Let me never forget to pray and read your word daily.

Continue to fill my soul with your precious Holy Spirit. Watch over my children. Give us rest from our fears so we can serve you wholeheartedly. Whatever it is that we're lacking fulfill in us. May our family grow closer to you in Jesus Name Amen.

Epilogue: For those of you who may be reading this book but do not know the Lord. Ask him to come into your heart. Ask the Lord to take away anything that is hindering you from drawing nearer to know him. Don't be afraid to tell God I need you, I love you, I adore you, I worship you. Lord you are Master over my life. Fill me with your Holy Spirit change my way of life from this day forward In Jesus Name Amen

Letter to God

Dear God, I am releasing everything from my past to you today. I ask that you revive all things in me that have died. I repent of my sins and I ask you to regenerate my soul. Lord transform me into what you want me to be. I reverence you as I am reborn in you. Nothing the enemy can do will stop me from loving you because you love me for who

I am. There's nothing that anyone can say or do that will change this fact. Jesus stretched out his arms out on the cross signifying "I Love You This Much". I receive your love for me God in Jesus Name Amen

Single Saved -and- Satisfied

Darlyn Ellen Paris Campbell

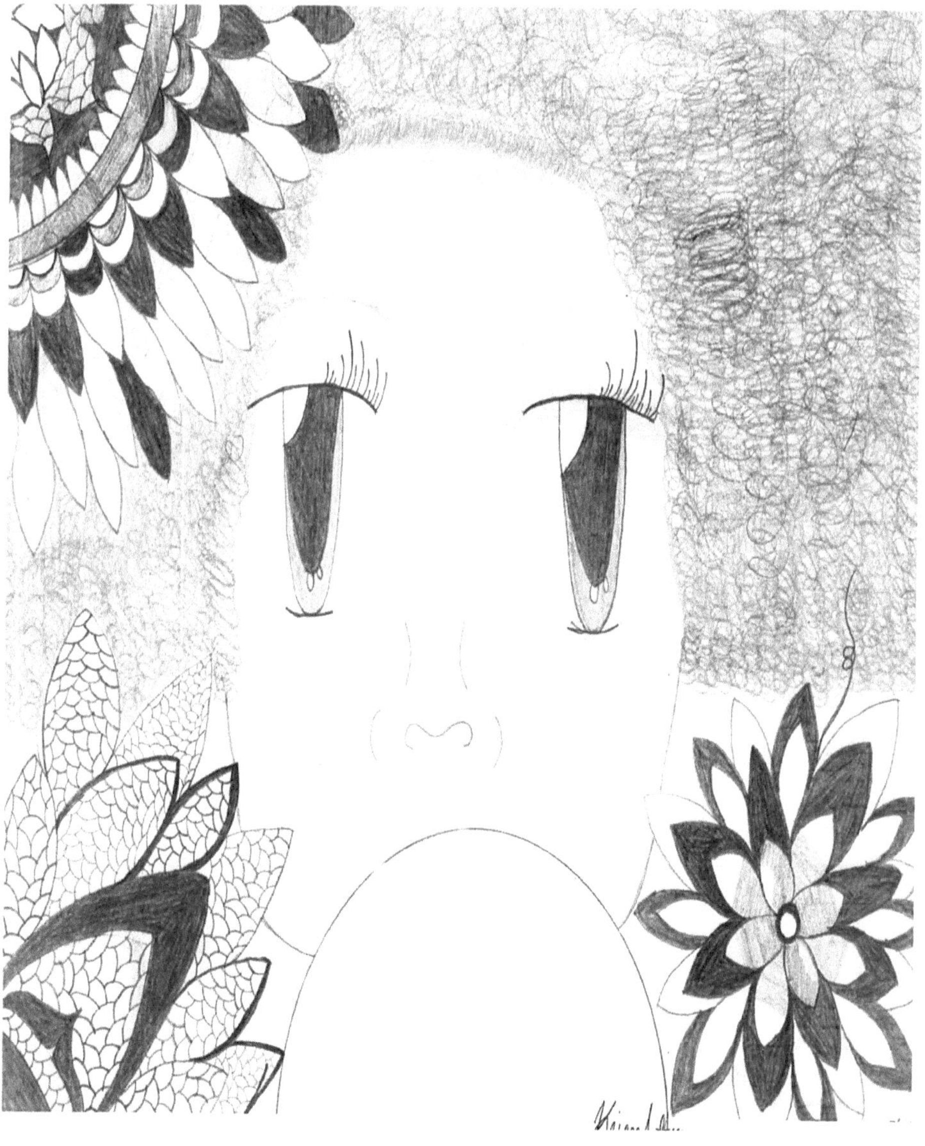

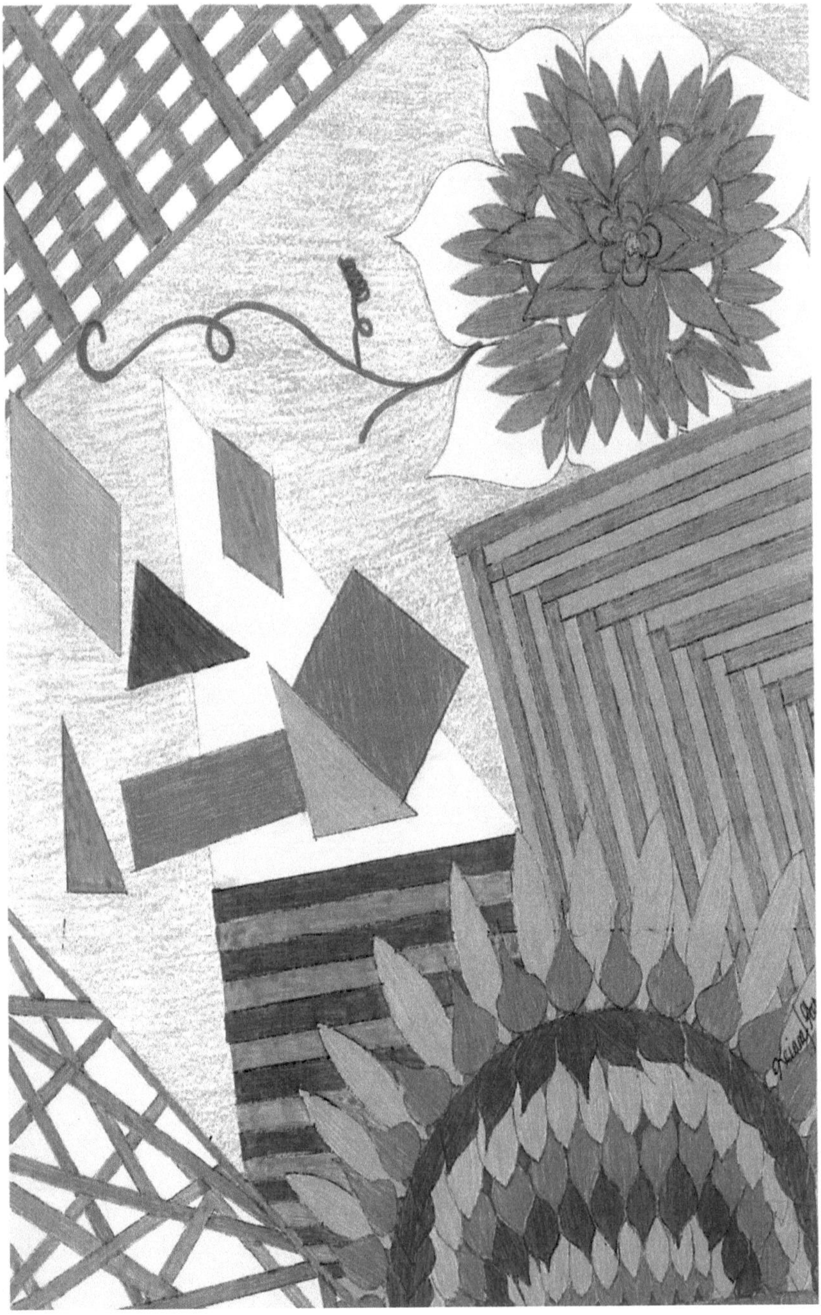